I Am More Than My Nightmares

A sequel to
I Am More Than a Daydream

by Jennae Cecelia

I Am More Than My Nightmares

ISBN: 978-1986217194

Cover art by Islam Farid
www.IslamFarid.net

Illustrations by Rylie Moran
Instagram: @gabriellescrapart

Dear Reader,

I have spent so much time sitting and envisioning some of my worst nightmares coming to life. While also avoiding countless moments because I overthink the outcomes.

I play nervously with my hair and get quiet when I think people are staring. But I have learned over the past few years how to better handle the worry and fear that lives in my mind.

I am not perfect. I still worry and I am still anxious, but I know that I am more than my nightmares.

If you are an anxious being and stumble across this, please know you are not alone.

I Am More Than My Nightmares is my journey from being engulfed in fear to learning how to let my mind free when it is calling for a break.

All of my love,
Jennae

I Am More Than My Nightmares

~

I had dreams
to climb mountains
I didn't even
know existed.
That is faith.

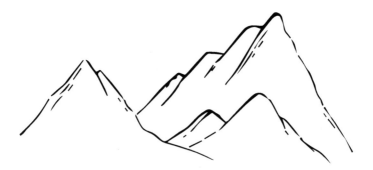

I am not sure
if the sun will
peak out for
me today,
or hide behind
the clouds.
But I know I will
see the light
again soon.
I will.

I am the tree
that stands through
a hurricane
even when I have been
pushed past my
breaking point.
Don't you see why
I would worry about
being hit by another
wave and not have
the strength
to stay standing?

I fear things
I know I will
never face,
yet I fear them
anyways.
That's anxiety.

How do I explain
that I can't go out
with you because
I am afraid of
the crowd
around us?
Afraid of the germs.
Afraid of the stares.
Afraid of the possibility
of not coming home.
How do I explain
that I am made up
of *FEAR*?

I see myself
as scribbles
on pages
longing to be
even lines.

It is
scary to be
a dreamer in
a world that
sees dreams
as only
small possibilities.

Have you ever
sat in a parking lot
after going through
the drive-thru,
and ate a bagel
smothered in cream cheese
because you couldn't eat
inside out of fear of the
judgment from people?
Even though they
are probably deep
in conversation
not even noticing
you or your choice
of food.
But what if they do?
What if they judge?
What if they stare?
What if?
What if?
What if?

Today may not be
my day,
but I have 364
to make better.

Fear comes like waves.
It never fully goes away.
Some waves are much
bigger than others,
but I have learned
to take more breaths
and talk about what is
swimming around
in my mind.
Then my fear
can start to subside.

Self-love is a
journey with
ever-changing
scenery.

There is fear
in traveling a path
that I have
never seen.
But here I am
doing it anyway
just to show up
my anxiety.

You are waiting
for this
rainy,
dreary,
season to change.
But just know
when it does,
you will
thank the clouds
for all they
taught you
and for all the growth
you gained.

I always have the fear
of my arms
not being
long enough
to protect everyone
that I love.

I want you
to comfort me,
but how do you
ease a heart
that never stops
racing and knees
that never stop
shaking,
even when asleep?

I fear my own voice.
It shakes
when I am scared.
It babbles
when I am nervous.
It stutters
when I am confused.
I fear my own voice,
so I write.

I have stared at
these same four walls.
Laid under the
same gray sheets.
I have memorized
the floor creeks.
I am scared to leave
this space
because it is so
comforting.
But how do I even
evict my mind anyway?

You wake up
to the sun
trying to peak
through your blinds.
It is ok to open them
and let the light in.
But do it when you
feel the time is right.

My mind is anxious,
but my soul
longs for peace.

I am not guaranteed
a week,
a month,
or a year.
I am not guaranteed
to get old enough
to see my face wrinkle
and my hair gray.
But I am guaranteed
right now,
this moment.
I will not live my life
betting on the next day.
I won't.
I will live for today.

I was watering
a plant every day
hoping for it to grow
and thrive.
I gave it love
and appreciation,
but my efforts saw
nothing in return.
Then one day
I realized the plant
I was worried about
helping live
the best life,
was just a fake one
for display only.

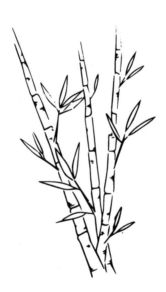

There are pieces of me
scattered all around,
and every time I try
to pick myself up again
there is another
gust of wind
that forces me
to start over.
But I will keep going.
I will.

All I want is to
run freely amongst
the wildflowers
and the trees.
I am tired of running
from my anxiety.

I see mountains
in the distance
that I long to climb.
But first I must
pack up my fear
and leave it behind.

The future has fog
on the horizon,
but there are
mountain peaks
and treetops
still in sight.
So don't give up
hope that there
will be clearance.

I've thought about
this moment
100 times over
in my head.
Played out every
possible scenario
that could have,
should have,
would have happened.
And I was still wrong.

Don't fear
the leaves changing.
For it is leading you
to the best season
of your life yet.

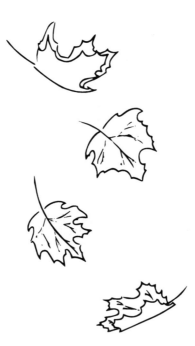

My anxious mind
worries about
what I am not being,
or what I should
be seeing.
My anxious mind
takes no vacation.

I was abandoned
in a forest
with no map,
no compass,
no water,
or food.
I sat down and
gave up because
how would I ever
make it out?
But if I had climbed
to the top of a tree
I would have seen
that not far off
in the distance
was victory.

I have gone down
rivers with still waters,
and rivers with rapids.
But I keep paddling
no matter how far
of a distance.

I looked into
the eye of my hurricane
and still managed to make
the most beautiful sunset.

You have plucked apart
my mind,
my body,
and my words.
Now that I let you go,
I remember who I was
at the core,
soulfully beautiful.

Even in dark times
there is opportunity
for beauty to rise,
like a lotus
from the mud.

Healing isn't taking
the fast lane
down the highway.
Healing is taking
back roads
with potholes
and dead ends.
But I will get there.
I will.

My version
of overcoming
my fears
might not be as
risky
or fearless
as jumping out
of an airplane
arms wide open.
But I am still facing
things that are just
as equally scary
to me.
Like starting up
a conversation
with the random stranger
next to me in line
to get coffee.

Treat people
like you would treat
your garden.
Care for them.
Be kind to them.
Nourish them.
Be forgiving if they
don't grow
the way you
would have liked.
Everyone is trying
their best to grow
through all the seasons
of their life.

Happy.
Happy.
Happy.
Happy.
Happy.
Happy.
Happy.
Happy.
If I say it enough
will it come true?

Somehow I was
that six-year-old
kid again.
Standing at the top
of the basement stairs
afraid of what would
await me at the bottom.
Nothing.
Nothing was there.
But oh did the fear
feel so real.

I am just trying
to be the woman
my fifteen-year-old self
would have admired.

I am jumping
off the pier
into the ocean,
ready to brave
all the water
in my face.
I will rise
to the top.
I will rise.

Although it seems
long and tiring,
one day you will
look back
and realize
all the growth
you made
on your hike.

There are vines
in my mind
that I am still
untangling.
But I will.

One time I planted
a whole garden
and expected
my fruit to
grow in abundance
and my flowers
to be full of color.
But a frost came
and took away
all of my hard work.
So I chose to plant
myself a new garden,
rather than give up
and be left in the dirt.
What would you have chosen?

The sun is getting ready
to create the most beautiful
sunrise for you.

I now stop
and greet
my reflection
instead of looking
past the girl
in the mirror.
All she ever wanted
was her own love.

I am the river moving
in the dead of winter.
Still pushing through strong
even when conditions
are at their worst.

I don't need
your hand
to coddle me,
I just need your
hand to say
I will be here,
fearlessly
and forever yours.

I am throwing
sticks in the air
and hoping
they land
as flower petals.

My journey has not
been perfect.
If it was,
I wouldn't
have been
crafted into
the woman
I am today....

STRONG.

BEAUTIFUL.

KIND.

GRATEFUL.

LOVING.

I will rise from
my soil
with beauty
and grace.

Does the earth
have anxiety too,
that maybe one day
she won't rotate
like she used to?
Or that her
valleys
and rivers
won't be cared for?

What if I grow
into a flower
you weren't expecting?
Would you still want
me in your garden,
or would you uproot
me like the rest?
I am longing for
a safe place to grow.

If the pieces
don't fall into place,
maybe it is time
to build yourself up
in a new
unconventional way.

Where there is
destruction,
pour light into it.

She can't stay
spring forever.
Her leaves will fall,
her air will chill.
But change is just
what she needs to
heal and rebuild.

All I need is to
throw my seeds
into the wind
and trust
the universe
will have me bloom
where I belong.

Don't worry about
the rivers you have
yet to cross.
Your body will
support you,
your wisdom will
guide you,
and your soul will be there
to hold your hand
if you ever start
to sway.

Mistakes are
the bridges
between
my failures
and my successes.

Forgive yourself, please.
Forgive yourself, please.
Three words
your body,
mind,
and soul need.

I would tape
motivational quotes
to my mirror
to remind
myself of the words
I couldn't always hear.

I see stars
as small reminders
from the universe
that even dark times
show specks
of light
when you really
pay attention.

I poured my
heart and soul
into you
until you were flooded
with me.
And you still didn't notice
even a drop of my water.

Just watch me grow
when I give myself
more of my love.

You can appreciate
the flowers in
someone else's
garden,
while still
watering
your own.

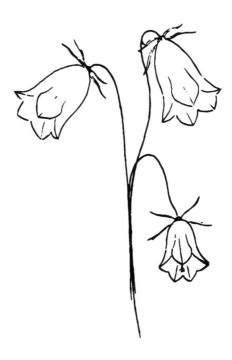

I have yet to explore
everywhere,
but I have at least
passed my comfort zone.

There is still beauty
behind the gray skies.
There is still beauty
in you.

I am an ocean.
Are you willing to
risk swimming in
the deep,
dark,
parts of me?
Or will you stay
where it's shallow?

You put up a wall,
but I can still see
your light through
the cracks.

If someone hasn't
told you lately
then I will.
You are the moon
lighting up
a dark room
and the sunrays
on my face.
You are a light
that is shining and
I appreciate you.

I lit my soul's candle.
Now I am glowing.

I am the clearing
in the forest
you have been
looking for.
Let my light guide
you out.

You are looking at
one of her chapters.
You don't know
her full story.

We are two people
on separate paths
that never intersect
no matter how many times
we long to cross paths
for even a few steps.

I am plunging
into cold water
that I once would have
tiptoed out to
only waist deep.
I won't let fear
drown me.

Make today
the day
you uncover
the dream
living deep,
down,
inside of you.

Although your branches
have been bare
for so long,
I see your buds
starting to grow.
Once they start
there is no
stopping you.

I once was walking
down a path
that only had a few feet
of clearance
and mud at my feet.
Now I am walking
down a clear path
filled with flowers,
and now my mind
is more at ease.

For the first time
in awhile I am
not swimming with
my arms in constant
motion and my
feet kicking
to stay afloat.
I am lying on top
of the unknown,
which scares me most.
Arms wide open,
eyes closed,
just simply breathing.

Sometimes our winters
flow unexpectedly
into our springs.
But hope,
hope will get you
through it.

There is a reason
your success
can't always
come quickly.
Haven't you ever
seen what happens
when too much of
anything happens
at once?
There is a flood.

We all have bad yesterdays
that we can bask in.
But those yesterdays
will never come again
and neither will
the today you are
wasting with thoughts
of your yesterdays.

I am grateful
for every storm
the universe
has given me.
I am who I am
because of every
raindrop
I have felt
and every gust
of wind that
has shifted me
in a different
direction.

The moon appears
even during the day
to let you know it is still
there and is
coming back soon.
Will you be my moon?
Because I am always
worried about you
when you are not around.

Your soul is waiting
for you to feed it
with all of your
wildest dreams.

It is scary
to open my heart
to someone I have
no control over.
Please treat
my heart like it is
your own.

Self-care is sometimes
just waking up,
greeting the sun,
and telling yourself
this is your day.

You are walking
around looking for
a path to follow
in the right direction.
The problem is,
the path you are
looking for
has not yet
been made.

Some days it feels
like I am talking
to a universe
with closed doors.
However, the universe
doesn't have any
doors to close.
It is always there,
open and listening.
Waiting for you
to catch on to
all the obvious signs
thrown your way.

It is hard
to grow
in this
2 x 4 box,
in the shade
with no water.
But this is
a test
of my limits,
and I will
grow outside
of the box if
I have to.

You say I
look different,
but the only
change in me
is now I am
looking at
myself
with a whole
new perspective.

Failure
elevates
my motivation.
Without failure
I am not
going to succeed.

It is not about
crossing the
finish line first,
while overworking
and stressing out
your body and mind.
It is about
making it in a way
that is most
caring to yourself.
Your mental health
is not a race.

People are
too worried about
themselves
to worry
about everything
you do.
I know it seems
like all eyes
are on you at times,
but sometimes
those eyes are
just blank stares
thinking about
their own problems.

My journey
is definitely not boring.
There are ruts
I have hit
and parts of me
that were lost.
But I know one day
when my journey
comes to an end,
I can say I felt
my strength in
the wind
and saw my soul
in the greenery.

Sometimes
I need a little
support.
Like a rope and
wooden stake
holding up a tree
that can't stand
quite right by its
self yet.
Soon I will
rise just fine
on my own.

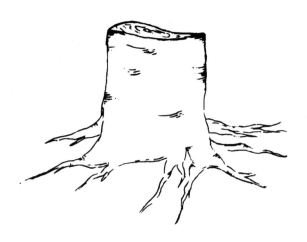

Do not fear,
the rain is
only here
to help you
grow.

Everyone has
broken pieces.
Even the people
you think
are so beautiful,
so perfect,
so happy.
We are just a bunch
of broken people
wanting to feel
put together.

Four years ago
I was a budding seed
trying so hard to
push through
the dirt
thrown on top
of me.
Now I am a flower
in full bloom,
flourishing from
all the new soil
around me.

~

~

To my dreamers,

Thank you for always
believing in me.

I hope if you have ever had anxious
tendencies, these poems help you
feel a little more at peace.

This book is meant to be
flipped through when
your anxious mind
needs some time to unwind
and realize, you are not alone.

Looking to read more of Jennae's books?

Here are her other books:

Bright Minds Empty Souls

Uncaged Wallflower

I Am More Than a Daydream

Uncaged Wallflower- Extended Edition

You can find them all on:

www.Amazon.com

www.barnesandnoble.com

www.bookdepository.com

About the Author

JennaeCecelia.com

Instagram: @JennaeCecelia

Jennae Cecelia is the self-published and best-selling author of multiple poetry books. I Am More Than My Nightmares is her fifth book and is a sequel to I Am More Than a Daydream.

She has developed a strong passion
for writing uplifting poetry that encourages her readers to reach their full potential and learn about fulfilling their dreams.

Jennae's soul is happiest when she is meditating, doing yoga, drinking coffee, exploring nature, drawing, or being around people who lift up her spirits.

Made in the USA
Middletown, DE
01 September 2018